SEASONAL LEARNING ACTIVITIES

WRITTEN BY THE STAFF AT THE LEARNING EXCHANGE—NATALIE BARGE, DARLENE BRANDTONIES, CONNIE CAMPBELL, BEVERLY CLEVENGER, PAT COOK, JENNY ISENBERG, DEBBI LEHR, PATTY LORING, SIDNEY MARTIN, MARY JANE MITCHELL, ELAINE MONDSCHEIN, CONNIE RACER, AND DYREESE SWEENEY.

COMPILED BY PATTY LORING
EDITED BY SIDNEY MARTIN

ILLUSTRATED BY PEGGY MURRAY

Cover by Peggy Murray

Copyright © Good Apple, Inc., 1988

GOOD APPLE, INC.
BOX 299
CARTHAGE, IL 62321-0299

Copyright © Good Apple, Inc., 1988

ISBN No. 0-86653-435-0

Printing No. 987654321

GOOD APPLE, INC.
BOX 299
CARTHAGE, IL 62321-0299

TABLE OF CONTENTS

BACK-TO-SCHOOL TRICKS 1

Interview Scramble 2
Casino Math 4
Mystery Person in the News 6
Welcome Word Search 8
Sign Your Team 10

HALLOWEEN TREATS 13

Fortune Telling 14
Favorite Costume Graph 16
Treat Bags 19
Spooky Puzzle 23

THANKSGIVING GOODIES 25

Fraction Dice 26
Thanksgiving Facts and Opinions 28
Turkey Hunt 32
Pilgrim Visitor 34

HOLIDAY DELIGHTS 37

Holiday Symbols 38
Singo 43
Holiday Puzzle Race 47
My True Love 48

WINTER GEMS 49

Winter Travelers 50
Average Height 54
Odd/Even Relay 55
Season Hunt 56

HEARTY AMERICA 61

Valentine Syllables 62
Presidential Press Conference 64
Valentine Board Race 67
Unusual Romances 70

ST. PAT'S GOLD MINE 73

Famous Sayings 74
St. Patrick's Memory Game 76
Catch the Lie 79
March Math Problems 80
St. Patrick's Dictionary Hunt 84

EASTER TREASURES 85

Mama's Baby 86
Rabbit Robot Road Relay 90
Eggs in a Bag 92

SPRING SUNSHINE 95

Mother Nature's Gameboard 96
Crazy Phrases 98
Funtoons 101
Spring a Riddle on Me 102
May Shapes 106

INTRODUCTION

Designed for educators of children from second through sixth grades, *Seasonal Learning Activities* is a unique source of clever educational activities that make learning fun. This book is packed with fresh, easy-to-prepare games, bulletin boards, and learning centers. Since the activities require only simple, inexpensive materials, many rich learning experiences can be provided at little cost. Because the activities are both fun and educational for children, *Seasonal Learning Activities* is perfect for classroom teachers, room parents, and youth group leaders.

Seasonal Learning Activities is organized into nine chapters, one for each month of the school year. Each chapter contains a medley of activities that encircle the curriculum strands.

All of the activities teach, reinforce skills that have been taught, or inspire creativity. "Famous Sayings," for example, entices students to use dictionaries and thesauruses. "Favorite Costume Graph" and "March Math Problems" challenge students' problem-solving abilities. "Pilgrim Visitor" is an appealing activity that stimulates creative thinking and writing.

The ideas in *Seasonal Learning Activities* were developed by the staff at The Learning Exchange, a not-for-profit teacher resource center in Kansas City, Missouri. During The Learning Exchange's fifteen-year history, we have found that educators are continuously searching for new ideas to use in their work with children. Through this book we hope to help meet that need.

BACK-TO-SCHOOL TRICKS

INTERVIEW SCRAMBLE

PURPOSE: Students will conduct interviews in order to learn more about each other.

MATERIALS:
1 copy of the Scrambled Interview Sheet for each student
Pencils
Bulletin boards

TEACHER PREPARATION:
1. Prepare the bulletin board.
2. Make a copy of the Scrambled Interview Sheet for each student.
3. Have the students pair off.
4. Give students directions.
5. After the interviews are completed, staple all the sheets to the board.

STUDENT DIRECTIONS:
1. Interview your partner and fill out the sheet for him. Do not write his name on the sheet.
2. Turn in the sheet to your teacher.
3. When the sheets are on the bulletin board, read each sheet. Try to guess whose it is.
4. Write your guess on each sheet.
5. After all guesses have been made, tally the guesses on your own sheet. How many people guessed your sheet correctly?

SCRAMBLED INTERVIEW SHEET

Hair color: _____   Usual mood: _____

Eye color: _____   Favorite color: _____

Height: _____   Favorite food: _____

Shoe size: _____   Favorite subject: _____

Number of brothers and sisters: _____

Number of pets: _____

Favorite restaurant: _____

Birthday month: _____

Favorite flavor of ice cream: _____

Address: _____

Telephone number: _____

I think this sheet belongs to:

_____   _____   _____
_____   _____   _____
_____   _____   _____
_____   _____   _____
_____   _____   _____
_____   _____   _____
_____   _____   _____
_____   _____   _____

Tally:

1._____ #_____

2._____ #_____

3._____ #_____   This sheet really belongs to:

4._____ #_____   _____

CASINO MATH

PURPOSE:	Students will review basic addition facts.
MATERIALS:	1 deck of playing cards Copy of directions
TEACHER PREPARATION:	1. Prepare a small table for 3-4 students. 2. Place the materials on the table.

STUDENT DIRECTIONS:	1. Players take turns being the dealer.
	2. The dealer gives each player one card facedown and one card faceup.
	3. The players peek at their facedown cards and total their points:
	    Face cards = 10 points
	    Aces = either 1 or 11 points
	    Number cards = face value
	4. The dealer then asks each player in turn if he wants another card. The player may have as many cards as he wants but must not get over 21 points.
	5. When the dealer has served the players, they all show their cards.
	6. The player who comes the closest to 21 points without going over wins. More than one player can win.

MYSTERY PERSON IN THE NEWS

PURPOSE: Students will identify the name of a person prominent in the news.

MATERIALS:
Small bulletin board
Desk or small table
Shoe box
Con-Tact paper
Paper
Pencils

TEACHER PREPARATION:
1. Prepare a small bulletin board similar to the one shown.
2. Place a desk or small table in front of the bulletin board.
3. Cut a slit in the top of the shoe box. Cover the box with Con-Tact paper, leaving the slit open.
4. Provide small sheets of paper and pencils.
5. Each week, post on the bulletin board a picture of a person who is prominent in the news.
6. Plan an award or other recognition for the students who correctly name the Mystery Person each week.

STUDENT DIRECTIONS:
1. Guess who the Mystery Person is.
2. Write your name and the name of the Mystery Person on a sheet of paper.
3. Put your paper into the box.
4. At the end of each week, the answers in the box will be checked.

VARIATIONS:
*Require the students to spell the name of the Mystery Person correctly.

*Have the students take turns providing pictures for the Mystery Person bulletin board.

WELCOME WORD SEARCH

PURPOSE: Students will use their visual skills to find and learn names of their classmates.

MATERIALS: Copy of the word search puzzle
Pens, fine-line markers, or colored pencils

TEACHER PREPARATION:
1. Write the first names of all of the students in the space around the word search puzzle.
2. In the boxes, write each student's name in a straight line across, down, or diagonally, printing one letter per box.
3. Names can intersect like a crossword puzzle.
4. When all of the names have been written in the puzzle, fill in any empty boxes with random alphabet letters.
5. Make a copy of the puzzle for each student.

STUDENT DIRECTIONS:
1. Look for the names of the students in your class. The names are written across, down, and diagonally.
2. When you find a name, carefully circle it with a pen, fine-line marker, or colored pencil.
3. Put a small check by each name outside the puzzle after you have circled it in the puzzle.
4. See how many of the names you can find.

VARIATIONS:
*Include the names of teachers and other adults in the school building.
*Have students work in teams to complete the puzzle.

WELCOME WORD SEARCH

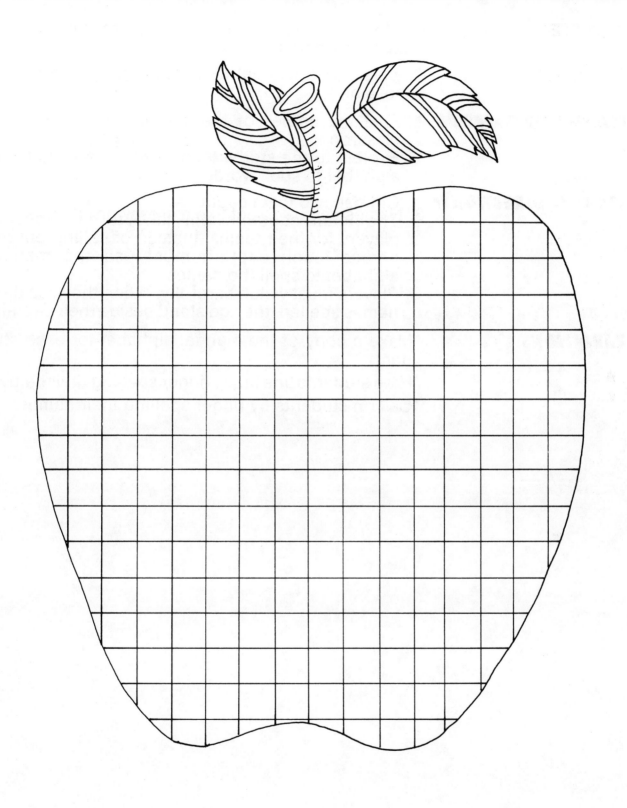

Name _____

SIGN YOUR TEAM

PURPOSE: Students will learn sign language as they choose teams for a game.

MATERIALS: Copies of the manual alphabet pages (enlarged, if possible)

TEACHER PREPARATION:
1. Post the copies of the manual alphabet in the classroom.
2. Explain to the students that deaf people use this alphabet to spell words.

STUDENT DIRECTIONS:
1. Choose two team captains.
2. The team captains will take turns choosing players for their teams. Instead of calling out the names, each captain must use the manual alphabet to spell the names.
3. Players must watch carefully. When they see their names spelled, they go stand beside their captain.

VARIATIONS:
*Make a copy of the manual alphabet for each student.

*Have students line up by finger spelling their names.

*Call on students by finger spelling their names.

SIGNING A PATTERN

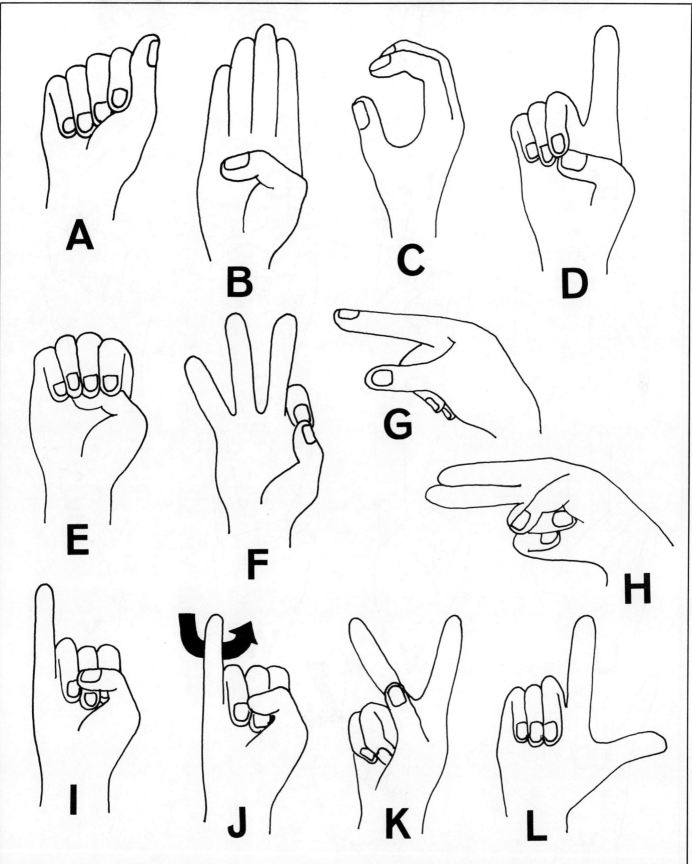

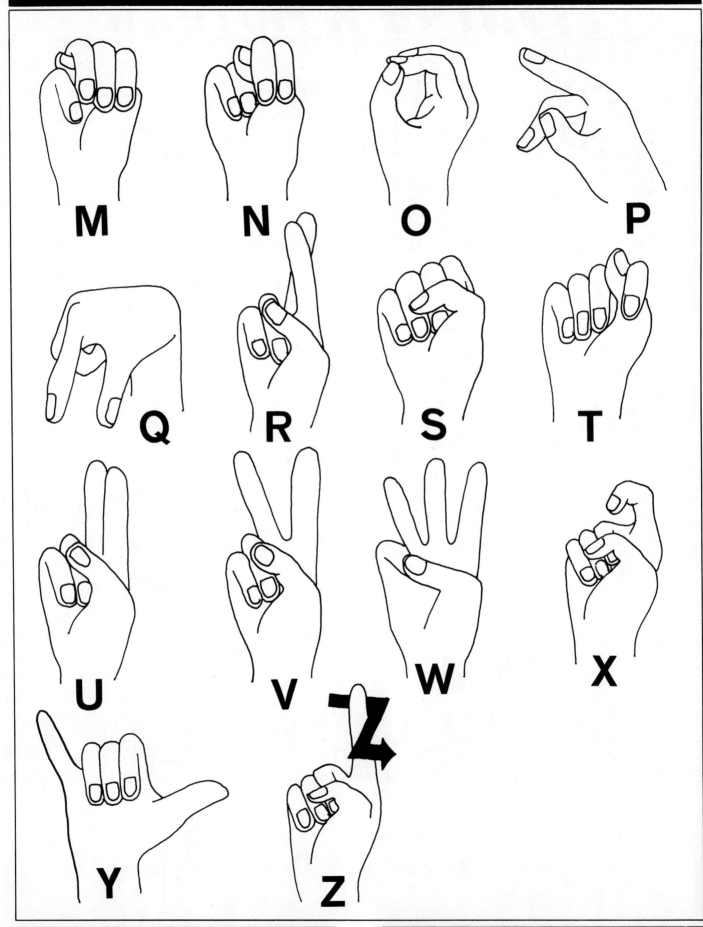

M N O P

Q R S T

U V W X

Y Z

FORTUNE TELLING

PURPOSE: Students will give words to complete a story.

MATERIALS: Copies of the Fortune Telling story
Pen or pencil

TEACHER PREPARATION:
1. Divide the class into small groups.
2. Designate one member of each group to be the group leader.
3. Give each leader a copy of the Fortune Telling story.

STUDENT DIRECTIONS:
1. The group leader should NOT show the Fortune Telling story to the other group members.
2. The leader asks the group for word suggestions and fills in the blanks in the story. Examples: "Give me a verb." "I need a noun."
3. The leader or a member of the group then reads the story aloud.

VARIATIONS:
*Have the groups of students follow up this activity by creating their own incomplete stories. Then the groups can exchange stories and complete them.

*Have each student write an incomplete story. Make enough copies of the stories for each child to compile a booklet of incomplete stories to take home.

FORTUNE TELLING
OR
(THE STORY OF _____'S LIFE)
(NAME OF PERSON IN GROUP)

_____ was born in a(n) _____ _____ to a family of
(NAME)   (ADJECTIVE)   (KIND OF BUILDING)

_____. Around _____, his/her family moved to
(NUMBER)   (DATE)

_____, where they made _____ for a living.
(CITY)   (OBJECT—PL.)

_____'s first girl/boyfriend was _____, but the couple
(NAME)   (OPPOSITE SEX NAME)

soon parted because _____ found _____'s
(NAME)   (OPPOSITE SEX NAME)

_____ so repulsive. In time, _____ grew to
(NOUN)   (NAME)

be _____ tall and decided to become a _____.
(MEASURE OF LENGTH)   (TYPE OF WORKER)

At the age of _____ he/she met the man/woman of
(NUMBER)

his/her dreams at a _____. Soon they married. Within _____
(PUBLIC PLACE)   (NUMBER)

_____ they had _____ children. The children all looked
(UNIT OF TIME—PL.)   (NUMBER)

like _____, since they had _____ hair,
(NAME)   (COLOR)

_____ noses and _____ toes on each foot. The family's
(ADJECTIVE)   (NUMBER)

fortunes were _____. In _____, _____ had _____
(ADJECTIVE)   (DATE)   (NAME)   (MONEY AMOUNT)

to his/her name. In later years he/she became famous for inventing a
_____ that could _____ itself. He/She is best remembered
(MACHINE OR TOOL)   (VERB)

today as being the first _____ to _____ on _____.
(LIVING THING)   (VERB)   (NAME OF A PLANET)

FAVORITE COSTUME GRAPH

PURPOSE: Students will graph their opinions and process information from the graph.

MATERIALS:
Large sheet of poster board
Markers
Copy of the student directions
Small sheets of paper
Bulletin board
Pins or tape

TEACHER PREPARATION:
1. On the poster board, use markers to draw three large interlocking circles. Label the circles as shown in the illustrations.
2. Mount the graph on a bulletin board. Post the copy of the student directions beside it.
3. If the students are not familiar with this form of graph, explain that each circle represents a description of a Halloween costume. The space where two circles overlap represents both descriptions. The space where all three circles overlap represents all three descriptions. Give several examples to show what different name placements would mean.
4. Give each student a small sheet of paper.
5. From the thought questions suggested, choose those that fit the students' abilities. After the graph is completed, use the questions to help students process the information.

STUDENT DIRECTIONS:
1. Write your name on your sheet of paper.
2. Think of your favorite Halloween costume.
3. Decide whether your favorite costume is scary, funny, unusual, or any combination of those descriptions.
4. Find a place on the graph that matches your decision.
5. Pin or tape your name on the graph.

VARIATIONS:
*Have students draw their favorite Halloween costumes to illustrate their decisions.
*Have students suggest their own thought questions.
*Before students place their names on the graph, have them predict what they think the finished graph will look like.

SCARY

FUNNY

UNUSUAL

SUGGESTED THOUGHT QUESTIONS:

1. How many students chose a scary costume?
2. How many students chose a funny costume?
3. How many students chose an unusual costume?
4. How many thought their costumes were scary and funny?
5. How many thought their costumes were funny and unusual?
6. How many thought their costumes were scary and unusual?
7. How many thought their costumes were scary, funny, and unusual?
8. What is the total number of student names on the graph?
9. How many more students chose scary costumes than unusual ones? Funny ones?
10. What percentage of students thought their costumes were funny? Scary? Unusual?
11. If you add the percentages, why will they total more than 100%?
12. If you predicted what the finished graph would look like, how does your prediction compare with the actual graph?
13. If a name appeared outside the circles, what do you think that would mean?
14. How would you describe the average favorite costume?

TREAT BAGS

PURPOSE:	Students will match words with the Halloween words they come from.
MATERIALS:	6 treat bags with flat bottoms Scissors Glue 6 copies of the face Copy of the smiles Copy of the student directions 1 large envelope Small cards
TEACHER PREPARATION:	1. Cut out and glue a smile onto each face. 2. Glue each face to the side of a treat bag. 3. Glue the student directions to the envelope. 4. Write one word from the list on each card. Place the cards in the envelope. 5. Place the treat bags in a row on a table or staple them to a bulletin board. 6. Place the envelope beside the bags.
STUDENT DIRECTIONS:	1. Choose a card from the envelope. Read the word. 2. Look at the letters in the word. Then look at the Halloween words on the treat bags. 3. Find the Halloween word that contains all of the letters on the card. Place the card in the bag. 4. Continue until you have matched each card to the right bag. 5. Watch out for "trick" words that do not match any bag. Set those cards aside.
VARIATIONS:	*Have students make their own word cards. *Have students list words that may fit more than one treat bag.

CUT

JACK-O-LANTERN

CUT

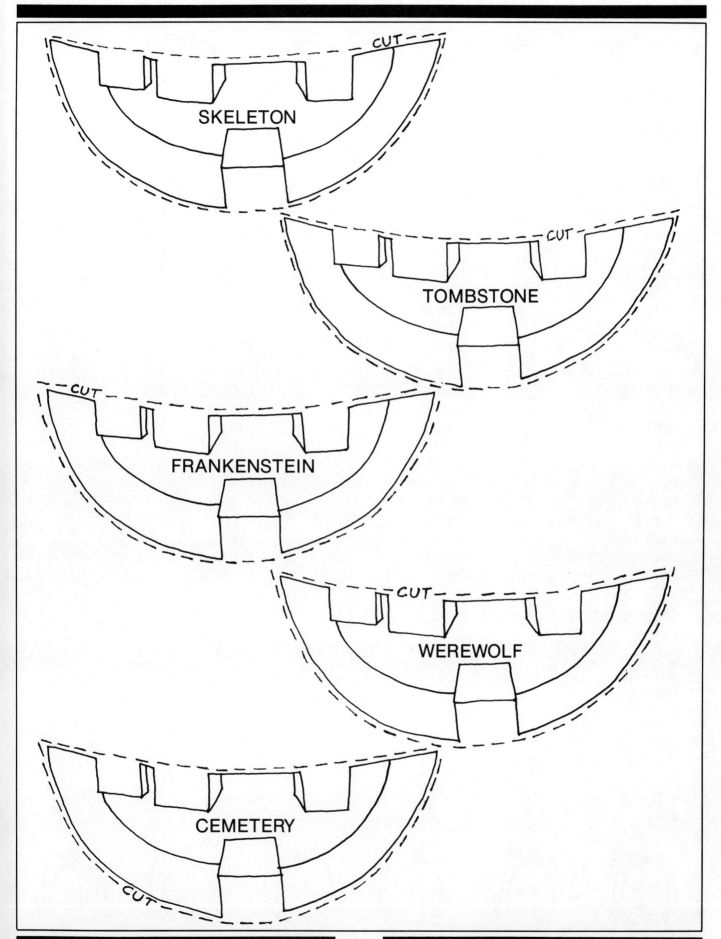

SKELETON

TOMBSTONE

FRANKENSTEIN

WEREWOLF

CEMETERY

CUT

CUT

CUT

CUT

CUT

WORD LISTS FOR TREAT BAGS

JACK-O-LANTERN	FRANKENSTEIN	SKELETON
loan	stain	lost
learn	risk	sleek
alert	tense	sleet
neck	rafts	stone
clank	snake	steel
jerk	nest	leek
later	sneaker	seen
carton	trains	kneel
antler	stink	seek
clean	strain	knee

WEREWOLF	TOMBSTONE	CEMETERY
flow	bones	meter
reel	most	meet
reef	note	term
feel	snob	rye
few	bottom	cry
fowl	botts	met
lower	mobs	try
flew	tone	yet
owl	some	teem
flower	best	emery

TRICK WORDS
witch
ghost
wicked
haunted

SPOOKY PUZZLE

Can you complete this?

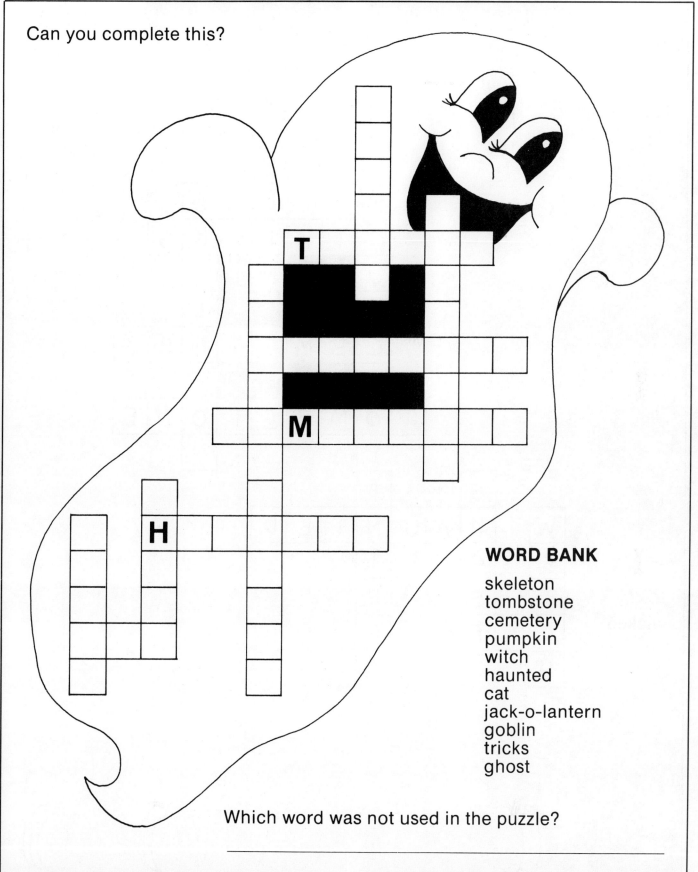

WORD BANK

skeleton
tombstone
cemetery
pumpkin
witch
haunted
cat
jack-o-lantern
goblin
tricks
ghost

Which word was not used in the puzzle?

_____

SPOOKY PUZZLE ANSWER KEY

THANKSGIVING GOODIES

TURKEY HUNT GRID

THANKSGIVING FACTS AND OPINIONS

4. Thanksgiving falls on the fourth Thursday of November.

5. The Pilgrim's famous feast occurred in the autumn of 1621.

6. The clothing that the Pilgrims wore was ugly.

FRACTION DICE

PURPOSE: Students will practice adding fractions.

MATERIALS:
Die pattern
Heavy paper or oaktag
Markers
Turkey pattern
Glue
Paper
Pencils

TEACHER PREPARATION:
1. Outline the die pattern twice on heavy paper or oaktag. Cut out both shapes.
2. Mark five sides of each die with fractions, such as $\frac{1}{2}$, $\frac{1}{4}$, $\frac{3}{8}$, $\frac{3}{4}$, and $\frac{1}{16}$.
3. Make two copies of the turkey pattern. Color both with markers and glue one onto the sixth side of each die.
4. Fold and glue the dice.
5. Copy the directions for the students.

STUDENT DIRECTIONS:
1. Two or three students may play.
2. Each player needs a sheet of paper and a pencil.
3. The first player rolls both dice and adds the fractions. Write the total on the paper.
4. Players take turns, keeping a running total on their papers.
5. A player who rolls a turkey can name its value. It can be any fraction less than 1 whole.
6. The first player to reach a total of 5 or more wins the game.

VARIATIONS:
*If students need to review addition facts, substitute whole numbers for fractions on the dice.

*Substitute decimals for fractions.

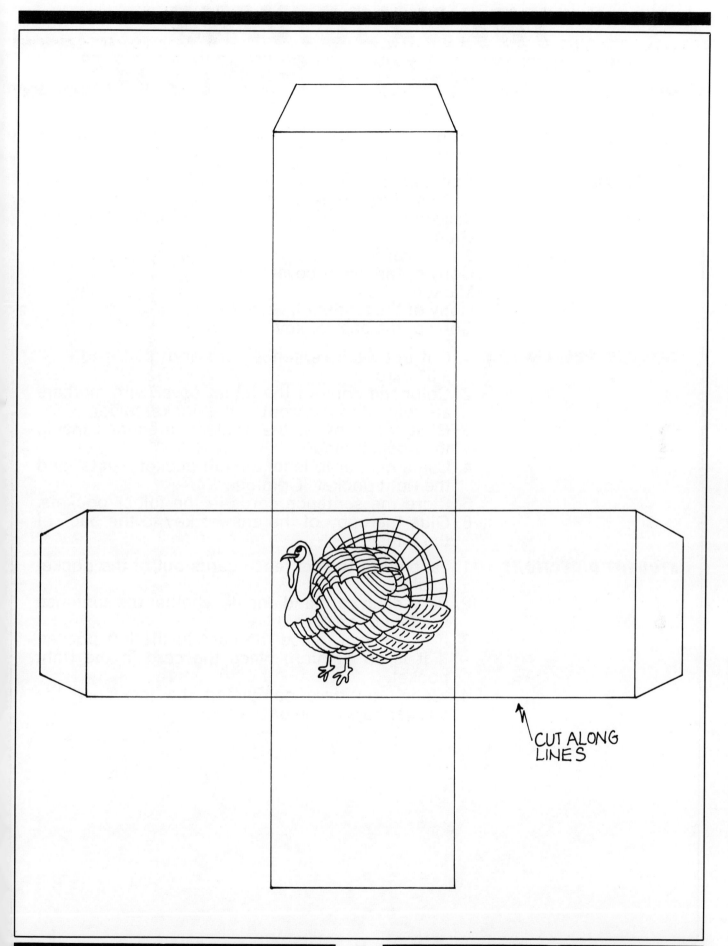

CUT ALONG
LINES

THANKSGIVING
FACTS AND OPINIONS

PURPOSE: Students will decide whether a statement is a fact or an opinion.

MATERIALS:
1 pocket folder
Copies of the sentence cards
Scissors
Glue
3" x 5" cards
Copy of the folder cover
Markers
Copy of the student directions
Copy of the answer key

TEACHER PREPARATION:
1. Cut out each sentence card and glue it to a 3" x 5" card.
2. Color the copy of the folder cover with markers and glue it to the front of the pocket folder.
3. Glue the copy of the student directions inside the pocket folder.
4. Use a marker to label the left pocket "Facts" and the right pocket "Opinions."
5. Store the sentence cards in the folder pockets.
6. Glue the copy of the answer key to the back of the folder.

STUDENT DIRECTIONS:
1. Take all of the sentence cards out of the pocket folder.
2. Read each card and decide whether the sentence is a fact or an opinion.
3. If it is a fact, place the card in the left pocket. If it is an opinion, place the card in the right pocket.
4. When you have completed the task, use the answer key on the back cover.

THANKSGIVING FACTS AND OPINIONS

SENTENCE CARDS FOR THANKSGIVING FACTS AND OPINIONS GAME

1. The first Thanksgiving was a harvest festival.

4. Thanksgiving falls on the fourth Thursday of November.

2. The best part of the Thanksgiving feast is the turkey.

5. The Pilgrims' famous feast occurred in the autumn of 1621.

3. A turkey roasting in the oven smells very good.

6. The clothing that the Pilgrims wore was ugly.

7. During their first winter in America, half of the Pilgrims died.

11. Turkey stuffing tastes better than mashed potatoes.

8. Thanksgiving is more fun than Halloween.

12. Everyone enjoys eating pumpkin pie with whipped cream.

9. Thanksgiving is an American holiday.

10. Wild turkeys like to eat corn.

ANSWER KEY FOR THANKSGIVING FACTS AND OPINIONS GAME

1. Fact
2. Opinion
3. Opinion
4. Fact
5. Fact
6. Opinion
7. Fact
8. Opinion
9. Fact
10. Fact
11. Opinion
12. Opinion

TURKEY HUNT

PURPOSE: Teams of students will work with a grid to find a hidden turkey.

MATERIALS:
Transparency
Overhead projector
Chalkboard
Chalk

TEACHER PREPARATION:
1. Make a transparency of the grid.
2. Place the transparency on the overhead projector. Project the grid onto the chalkboard.
3. Divide the class into two teams.
4. Choose one square in the grid to be the place where the turkey is hiding. Write the coordinates on a small sheet of paper to help you remember.

STUDENT DIRECTIONS:
1. The object of the game is to find the hidden turkey.
2. Team members must work together to decide in which square the turkey is located.
3. Teams take turns choosing a square by saying, for example, "We think the turkey is in square 4,D." One team member draws an X in that square on the chalkboard.
4. The teacher tells whether the guess is correct.
5. The next team must choose from the remaining squares.
6. The team that finds the turkey wins the game.

VARIATIONS:
*Draw the grid on a chalkboard, or draw it on poster board and then laminate it.

*Have student choose the square for the hidden turkey.

*Designate two or more adjoining squares as the hiding place for a larger turkey. The teams would have to identify all of the squares to find the turkey.

TURKEY HUNT GRID

	1	2	3	4	5	6
H						
G						
F						
E						
D						
C						
B						
A						

PILGRIM VISITOR

PURPOSE: Students will practice writing step-by-step directions.

MATERIALS:
3" x 5" cards
Copies of the task cards
Scissors
Glue
Copy of the student directions
1 large envelope
Pencils
Paper

TEACHER PREPARATION:
1. Cut out each task card copy and glue it to a 3" x 5" card. Laminate the cards if possible.
2. Glue the copy of the student directions to the front of the large envelope.
3. Store the task cards inside the envelope.
4. Provide pencils and paper for the students' responses.

STUDENT DIRECTIONS: When the Pilgrims arrived in this country, they learned much from the Indians. The Indians taught the Pilgrims how to hunt, to make simple tools, and to grow and fertilize new vegetables such as corn, squash, and pumpkins.

1. Pretend that a Pilgrim from that time has come to live near you. You will teach the Pilgrim how we do something today.
2. Choose a task card from the envelope and read it.
3. Using the paper and pencil, write step-by-step directions that tell how to do the task. Remember that the Pilgrim may know nothing about the task or the materials that are needed. Make your directions complete, explaining when necessary. If it would be helpful, draw and label a picture.
4. Read over your directions and make any changes needed.
5. Give your directions to a friend. See whether he can follow the directions.
6. Make any other changes necessary.
7. Give your directions to your teacher.

TASK CARDS FOR PILGRIM VISITOR

Change the channel on a television set.	Take a shower.
Order a meal at a fast-food restaurant.	Order pizza to go.
Use a microwave oven.	Wash dishes in a sink.
Ride a bicycle.	Make popcorn in a microwave oven.

Sharpen a pencil.	Make a tape recording.
Make a telephone call.	Play a video game.
Put on a plastic bandage.	Use a computer.
Change a light bulb.	Brush and floss teeth.

HOLIDAY DELIGHTS

HOLIDAY SYMBOLS

PURPOSE: Students will practice using visual memory skills.

MATERIALS:
Large sheet of poster board
Copies of the symbols
Markers
Glue
Paper
Pencils

TEACHER PREPARATION:
1. Color and cut out the symbols.
2. Glue the symbols onto the poster board.

STUDENT DIRECTIONS:
1. The teacher or leader shows the poster to the group for thirty seconds.
2. The students then have two minutes to write down the names of as many symbols as they can recall.
3. Exchange papers and check.

VARIATIONS:
*Have the students compile a group list on the chalkboard to see if all of the symbols can be named.
*Use the poster as a classroom holiday decoration after the game is played.

- - CUT - - -

CUT

CUT

CUT

CUT

CUT

CUT

CUT

CUT

CUT

CUT

CUT

CUT

SINGO

PURPOSE:	Students will review musical symbols.
MATERIALS:	1 copy of the blank Singo card for each student Markers 2 copies of the master sheet Heavy paper Glue 1 Ziploc bag Dried beans, macaroni, or other game markers

TEACHER PREPARATION:

1. To prepare each Singo card, draw the eight musical symbols in the twenty-four boxes at random. You will need to draw each symbol three times, but be sure not to repeat the same symbol in any column.
2. Glue one copy of the master sheet to heavy paper and laminate it, if possible. With the other copy of the master sheet, cut out all of the squares to use as calling cards during the game. Place these cards in the Ziploc bag.
3. Give each player a Singo card and a pile of game markers.
4. Choose a leader.

STUDENT DIRECTIONS:

1. The object of Singo is to cover a complete row of symbols with game markers. The row may be horizontal, vertical, or diagonal.
2. Each player places a game marker on the caroler in the middle of the card. This is the free space.
3. The leader draws a calling card and reads it to the class, telling the letter and the name of the symbol.
4. Each player looks in the letter column on the card to find the symbol called. If the symbol is there, the player covers it with a game marker.
5. The leader then places the card on the master sheet.
6. Play continues until a player has a complete row covered and calls out "Singo."
7. The leader checks the winner's row of covered symbols with the master sheet.
8. The winner leads the next game.

VARIATIONS:

*Have the students draw the symbols to make their own Singo cards.
*For younger players, make cards with fewer squares.

SINGO MASTER SHEET

S𝄽	I𝄽	N𝄽	G𝄽	O𝄽
S𝅝	I𝅝	N𝅝	G𝅝	O𝅝
S♯	I♯	N♯	G♯	O♯
S♭	I♭	N♭	G♭	O♭

♩ "Quarter note"

𝅗𝅥 "Half note"

𝄞 "Treble clef"

𝄢 "Bass clef"

𝄽 "Quarter rest"

𝅝 "Whole note"

♯ "Sharp"

♭ "Flat"

S	I	N	G	O

HOLIDAY PUZZLE RACE

PURPOSE: Students will work cooperatively to complete a puzzle.

MATERIALS: 4 holiday jigsaw puzzles with an equal number of pieces

TEACHER PREPARATION:
1. Divide the class into four teams.
2. Give each team a puzzle.

STUDENT DIRECTIONS:
1. Work as a team to put your puzzle together.
2. The first team to complete its puzzle wins the race.

VARIATIONS:
*Have the teams trade puzzles and repeat the process. Did the same team win?

*Mix the pieces of four different puzzles together on a table. Have each team choose a puzzle box. Have a team member gather and bring back to the team all of the pieces of their puzzle. Then the whole team puts it together.

*Mix the pieces of four different puzzles together. Divide the pieces equally among the teams. Direct the teams to negotiate with each other, trading pieces as necessary so that each team completes one puzzle.

*Instead of jigsaw puzzles, use holiday crossword puzzles or poems or carols with mixed-up lines or missing words.

MY TRUE LOVE

STUDENT DIRECTIONS:

How many gifts did my true love give to me? Work with a partner to find the answer. First, write the number of gifts named in each line. Then add those numbers to find the total.

MY TRUE LOVE GAVE TO ME:

NUMBER OF GIFTS:

A partridge in a pear tree _____

Two turtledoves _____

Three French hens _____

Four calling birds _____

Five gold rings _____

Six geese a-laying _____

Seven swans a-swimming _____

Eight maids a-milking _____

Nine ladies dancing _____

Ten lords a-leaping _____

Eleven pipers piping _____

Twelve drummers drumming _____

TOTAL _____

How does your answer compare with other answers in the class?

_____

Why do some of the answers vary? _____

_____

Your names: _____

_____

WINTER GEMS

WINTER
TRAVELERS

1. Molly Pepper went to Pittsburgh.

She packed: ... did not pack:
apples
puppies
carrots
rab...

3. Gloria Birmingham went to Chicago.

She packed: She did not pack:
petunias   windows
                tulips

6. Tracy Patrick traveled to Nebraska.

She packed: She did not pack:
presents   stars
neutrons   gifts
                flower
                stick

8. Lloyd McCoy traveled to Detroit.

He packed: He did not pack:
toys   keys
boiler   clothes
boy   robot
dolly   photographs

WINTER TRAVELERS

PURPOSE: Students will look for word patterns.

MATERIALS: 1 pocket folder
Copy of cover sheet
Copies of game cards
Copy of directions
Copy of answer key
3" x 5" note cards
Markers
Glue

TEACHER PREPARATION:
1. Color the copy of the cover sheet and glue it to the front of the pocket folder.
2. Glue each game card to a 3" x 5" note card. Laminate the cards, if possible.
3. Glue the directions to one of the pockets inside the folder.
4. Glue the answer key to the back of the folder.
5. Place the game cards in the pockets.

STUDENT DIRECTIONS:
1. Read each card.
2. Try to figure out why the person packed those particular things. Use your knowledge of word patterns.
3. Check your answers with the answer key on the back of the folder.

VARIATIONS:
*Have students add three items to each list of things to pack.
*Have students make up their own game cards using word patterns.

WINTER TRAVELERS

WINTER TRAVELERS' CARDS

1. Molly Pepper went to Pittsburgh.

She packed:	She did not pack:
apples	oranges
puppies	dogs
carrots	sacks
rabbits	grapes

2. Jake Gates traveled to Maine.

He packed:	He did not pack:
cane	brush
paints	piano
grapes	needle
hay	fish

3. Gloria Birmingham went to Chicago.

She packed:	She did not pack:
petunias	windows
gentlemen	tulips
strawberries	toothpaste
envelopes	hangers

4. Bev Smith traveled to Little Rock.

She packed:	She did not pack:
brushes	lions
lipstick	combs
clocks	corn
checks	ice cream

5. Dyreese Brooks went to Tallahassee.

She packed:	She did not pack:
broom	mirror
vacuum	records
books	bottles
cheese	peaches

6. Tracy Patrick traveled to Nebraska.

She packed:	She did not pack:
presents	stars
neutrons	gifts
gravel	flower
breakfast	stick

7. Shirley White went to Massachusetts.

She packed:	She did not pack:
wreath	poster
dishes	books
church	bowls
whales	pencils

8. Lloyd McCoy traveled to Detroit.

He packed:	He did not pack:
toys	keys
boiler	clothes
boy	robot
doily	photographs

9. Steven Smith went to Fresno.

   He packed: He did not pack:
   mask   fork
   snake   pencil
   stapler   fruit
   spoon   papers

10. Woodstock Coldsnow traveled to Springfield.

   He packed: He did not pack:
   popcorn   ornaments
   seashells   patterns
   fireworks   kitchens
   soapsuds   asparagus

11. Herbert Marshall went to Denver.

   He packed: He did not pack:
   girdle   film
   alarm   sandwich
   thorn   belt
   purse   bicycle

ANSWER KEY

The names of all the things packed have:

1. double consonants
2. long **a** sound
3. three syllables
4. short vowel sounds
5. double vowels
6. **r** blends
7. digraphs
8. **oi** and **oy** vowel diphthongs
9. **s** blends
10. compound words
11. **r**-controlled vowels

AVERAGE HEIGHT

PURPOSE: Students will practice finding averages.

MATERIALS: 6 to 8 sets of identical or similar objects (Examples: a box of paper clips, 12 unsharpened pencils, 10 shoes, 15 felt-tip markers, 40 wooden blocks, 10 lunch boxes)
Paper
Pencils

TEACHER PREPARATION:
1. Divide the class into teams of four or five students.
2. Give each team a sheet of paper, a pencil, and one set of objects.

STUDENT DIRECTIONS:
1. You will use your materials to find the average height of your team.
2. Have one team member lie on the floor. Place the objects end to end alongside the person.
3. Count the number of objects it takes to measure the person from head to heel.
4. Record the measurement on the paper.
5. Measure and record the height of each team member.
6. To find the average height, first add the heights together. Then divide by the number of team members.
7. Record your team's average height on the paper. (Example: "The average height of our team is five lunch boxes.")

VARIATIONS:
*Have the teams exchange sets of objects and compare the results.
*Find a class average for each measuring object.
*Have the students think of other objects to use for measuring.
*Have the students convert the average height to inches and centimeters.

ODD/EVEN RELAY

PURPOSE: Students will practice deciding whether a number is odd or even.

MATERIALS:
30, 3" x 5" cards
Green marker
Red marker
Chalkboard with a chalk tray
Chalk

TEACHER PREPARATION:
1. Use the red marker to write a different odd or even number on each of fifteen cards.
2. Make an identical set of fifteen cards using the green marker.
3. Prepare the chalkboard as shown.
4. Divide the class into two relay teams.
5. Give each team a set of cards.

STUDENT DIRECTIONS:
1. Each team forms a line, one player behind another, facing the chalkboard.
2. Stack the set of cards in front of the first player in each line.
3. When the teacher says, "Go," the first player on each team picks up one card. The player decides whether the number on the card is odd or even.
4. The player places the card on the chalk tray under the correct word.
5. If the card was placed correctly, the player moves quickly to the end of the team line. If not, the player must move the card to the correct place. The teacher is the referee.
6. Play continues until one team has correctly placed all of its cards on the chalk tray. That team wins the race.

VARIATIONS:
Make cards to sort according to other criteria:
*Living/nonliving things
*Goods/services
*Plants/animals
*Parts of speech
*Long/short vowels
*Synthetic/natural substances
*Sedimentary/igneous/metamorphic rocks
*Division problems with/without remainders

TEAM 1		TEAM 2	
ODD	EVEN	ODD	EVEN

SEASON HUNT

PURPOSE: Students will review the four seasons and work in teams to put a puzzle together.

MATERIALS: Copies of the season cards
Scissors

TEACHER PREPARATION:
1. Cut out the season cards and laminate them, if possible.
2. While the students are out of the room, hide all of the season cards around the room.
3. Divide the children into four teams.
4. Assign each team a work area and a season: spring, summer, autumn, or winter.

STUDENT DIRECTIONS:
1. You will hunt for season cards that are hidden around the room.
2. Each team member will search for cards that match the team's season.
3. When you find a season card, read the words on the card.
4. If the words match your season, take the card to your team's work area.
5. If the words match another team's season, replace the card where you found it.
6. Put the season cards together at your work area. If you have found all of your cards, they will form a picture puzzle.

VARIATIONS:
*Use the season cards as an individual activity in your science center.
*Design a set of cards that will help students review parts of speech.

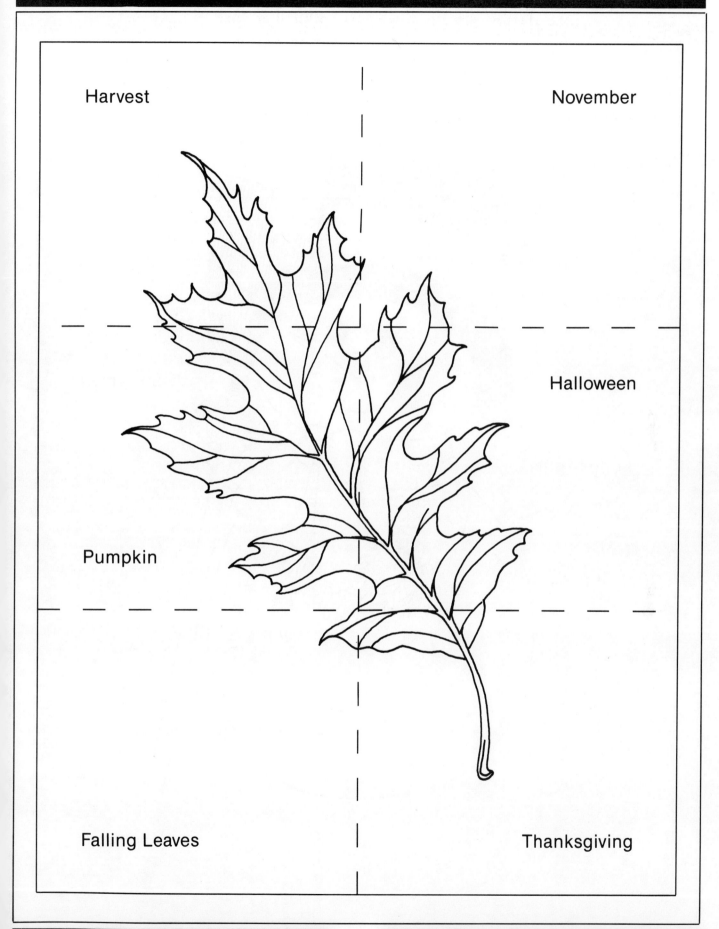

Harvest

November

Halloween

Pumpkin

Falling Leaves

Thanksgiving

Sleds

Scarves

Snowman

Long Nights

January

Valentines

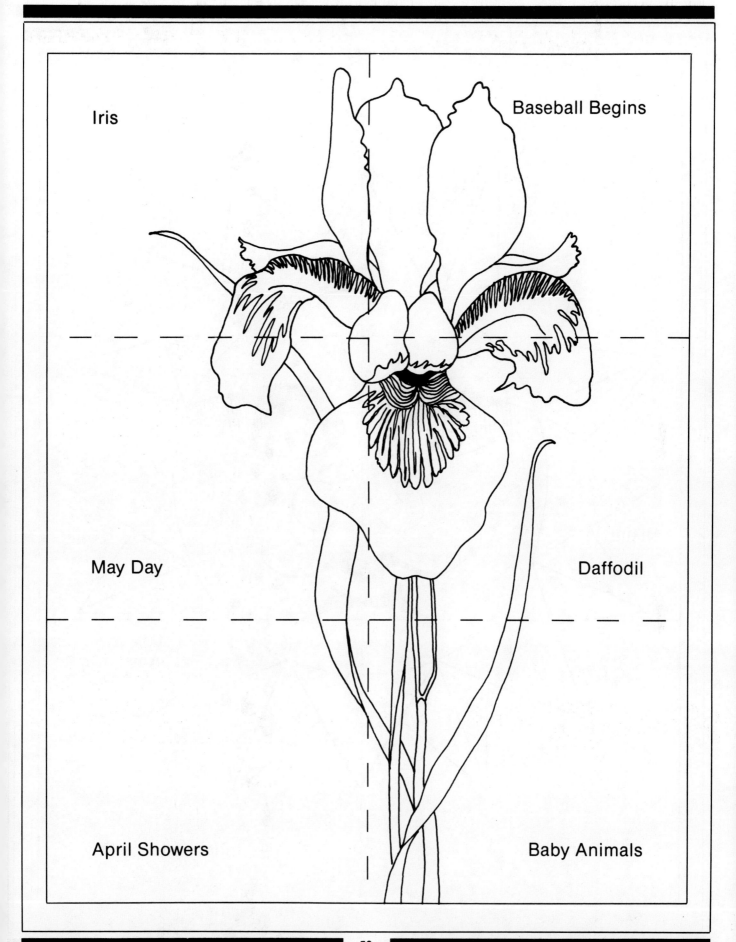

Iris

Baseball Begins

May Day

Daffodil

April Showers

Baby Animals

Long Days

August

Bikini

Beach

Hot Sun

Independence Day

VALENTINE SYLLABLES

PURPOSE:	Students will practice counting syllables in words.
MATERIALS:	Red construction paper Markers Scissors
TEACHER PREPARATION:	1. Copy or trace three hearts for each student on the construction paper. 2. Give each student a set of hearts, scissors, and a marker. 3. Have the list of valentine words available to read to the class.
STUDENT DIRECTIONS:	1. Cut out the three hearts. 2. Use your marker to write a large *1* on one heart, a *2* on another, and a *3* on the last heart. 3. Listen while your teacher reads a valentine word. 4. Decide whether the word has one, two, or three syllables. 5. Hold up your matching heart so that the teacher can check your answer.
VARIATIONS:	*Give each student a list of the words. Have the students write the number of syllables in the words. *Have the students use some of the words on the list to write stories.

heart	1	friends	1
valentine	3	exchange	2
cupid	2	share	1
love	1	romantic	3
arrow	2	affection	3
favorite	3	couple	2
sweetheart	2	crush	1
dance	1	smile	1
admirer	3	flirt	1
flowers	2	hugs	1
present	2	kisses	2
candy	2	darling	2
together	3		

PRESIDENTIAL PRESS CONFERENCE

PURPOSE: Students will review facts from the United States Constitution that relate to the President.

MATERIALS: 2 copies of the questions and answers
Scissors
Glue
1 small box

TEACHER PREPARATION:
1. From one copy of the questions and answers, cut out each question. (Do not include the answers.)
2. Put all of the questions in the box.
3. Explain to the students that they will role-play a presidential press conference.
4. Give the complete copy of the questions and answers to the student who volunteers to be the President. Allow the President time to study the questions and answers.
5. Have fifteen reporters each draw one question from the box.
6. After the press conference, divide the reporters into teams for follow-up news reporters.

STUDENT DIRECTIONS:
1. The President will stand in the front of the class and answer questions during the press conference.
2. The rest of the students, as reporters in the White House press corps, will take turns asking the questions.
3. When the President calls on a reporter, the reporter reads his question to the President.
4. The President answers the question and then calls on another reporter.
5. All press corps members must take notes during the press conference.
6. After the press conference, teams of reporters will prepare newspaper, television, or radio reports of their findings. The teams may gather further information from the Constitution and from other reference materials.

VARIATIONS:
*Students may develop their own questions.
*Students may take turns being the President.

PRESIDENTIAL PRESS CONFERENCE

QUESTIONS AND ANSWERS

QUESTION #1:   (Mr. or Ms.) President, how long is your elected term in office?

ANSWER #1:   Four years.

QUESTION #2:   (Mr. or Ms.) President, in what country were you born?

ANSWER #2:   I was born in the United States of America. All Presidents must be natural-born citizens.

QUESTION #3:   (Mr. or Ms.) President, how old do you have to be before you can become a President?

ANSWER #3:   At least thirty-five years old.

QUESTION #4:   (Mr. or Ms.) President, are you paid for being President?

ANSWER #4:   Yes, the Congress pays me a salary. During my term of office my salary cannot be increased or decreased, and I cannot receive any other salary from the United States or from any state.

QUESTION #5:   (Mr. or Ms.) President, what did you promise when you took the oath of office?

ANSWER #5:   I promised to preserve, protect, and defend the Constitution of the United States.

QUESTION #6:   (Mr. or Ms.) President, were you elected by the popular vote of the people?

ANSWER #6:   In reality, no. I was elected by a vote of the electors from each state.

QUESTION #7:   (Mr. or Ms.) President, who becomes President if you die or are removed from office?

ANSWER #7:   The Vice-President becomes President in that case.

QUESTION #8: (Mr. or Ms.) President, do you have any military powers?

ANSWER #8: Yes, I am commander in chief of the armed forces. I have great power, especially in time of war.

QUESTION #9: (Mr. or Ms.) President, can you make treaties?

ANSWER #9: Yes, I can, but all treaties must be approved in the Senate by a two-thirds vote of the senators present.

QUESTION #10: (Mr. and Ms.) President, who appoints important government officials?

ANSWER #10: I do, but they must be approved in the Senate by a majority of the senators present.

QUESTION #11: (Mr. or Ms.) President, in what branch of the government do you serve?

ANSWER #11: The executive branch.

QUESTION #12: (Mr. or Ms.) President, do you report to anyone?

ANSWER #12: Yes, I must report to the Congress from time to time on the state of the Union.

QUESTION #13: (Mr. or Ms.) President, can you be removed from office once you are the President?

ANSWER #13: Yes, I can be impeached if I am convicted of treason, bribery, or other serious crimes.

QUESTION #14: (Mr. or Ms.) President, if you are disabled, who carries out your duties?

ANSWER #14: If I am too ill or unable, I will assign those duties to the Vice-President. I will notify Congress in writing that the Vice-President will be Acting President until I am able to continue my duties.

QUESTION #15: (Mr. or Ms.) President, is there a limit to the number of terms you can serve as President?

ANSWER #15: Yes, I can only be elected President twice. This was not always the case, however.

VALENTINE BOARD RACE

PURPOSE: Students will read and follow directions.

MATERIALS:
1 copy of the gameboard
1 file folder
Glue
1 copy of the student directions
Markers
1 penny
3 to 4 game pieces

TEACHER PREPARATION:
1. Glue the copy of the gameboard to the inside of the file folder.
2. Glue the student directions to the bottom of the front cover.
3. Use a marker to write "Valentine Board Race" at the top of the front cover.
4. Color the blank hearts on the gameboard. Laminate the game, if possible.
5. Provide the penny and game pieces for the students.

STUDENT DIRECTIONS:
1. Three or four people may play this game. Each player takes a game piece and places it on Start Here.
2. The first player tosses the penny and moves ahead one space for "tails" or two spaces for "heads."
3. A player who lands on a space with directions must read them and do whatever they say.
4. Players take turns until one player lands on the winning space.

If you end up here, you get to use the Valentine Path.

Whisper to the other players and tell who you love.

Valentine Path

You are brokenhearted. Go back three.

Go ahead one and be my valentine.

You are a sweetheart. Let one player go ahead two. You choose.

Start Here

Heads = Go ahead 2.
Tails = Go ahead 1.

UNUSUAL ROMANCES

PURPOSE: Students will write stories.

MATERIALS:
1 copy of each heart
1 pocket folder
Marker
Scissors
Paper
Pencils

TEACHER PREPARATION:
1. Cut out the hearts. Laminate them if possible.
2. Using the marker, write "Unusual Romances" on the cover of the pocket folder.
3. Inside the folder, label the left pocket "Boys" and the right pocket "Girls."
4. Cut each heart in half.
5. Put the left sides of the hearts in the "Boys" pocket. Put the right sides in the "Girls" pocket.
6. Provide paper and pencils.
7. Display the completed stories with the heart halves on a bulletin board.

STUDENT DIRECTIONS:
1. Without looking, choose one heart half from the left folder pocket and another from the right pocket.
2. Read the name on each heart half. Imagine the unusual romance this couple would have.
3. Using the paper and a pencil, write a story that describes the couple's romance.
4. When you have finished your story, replace the heart halves in the correct pockets.

VARIATIONS:
*Have the students tell the stories instead of writing them.
*Have the students create some unusual romances of their own.
*Have students work in pairs to write the stories.
*Compile the completed stories into a class booklet.

Clark Kent | Lois Lane

CUT

Ken | Barbie

CUT

Popeye | Olive Oyl

CUT

Prince Charm-ing | Cinder-ella

CUT

Mickey Mouse | Minnie Mouse

CUT

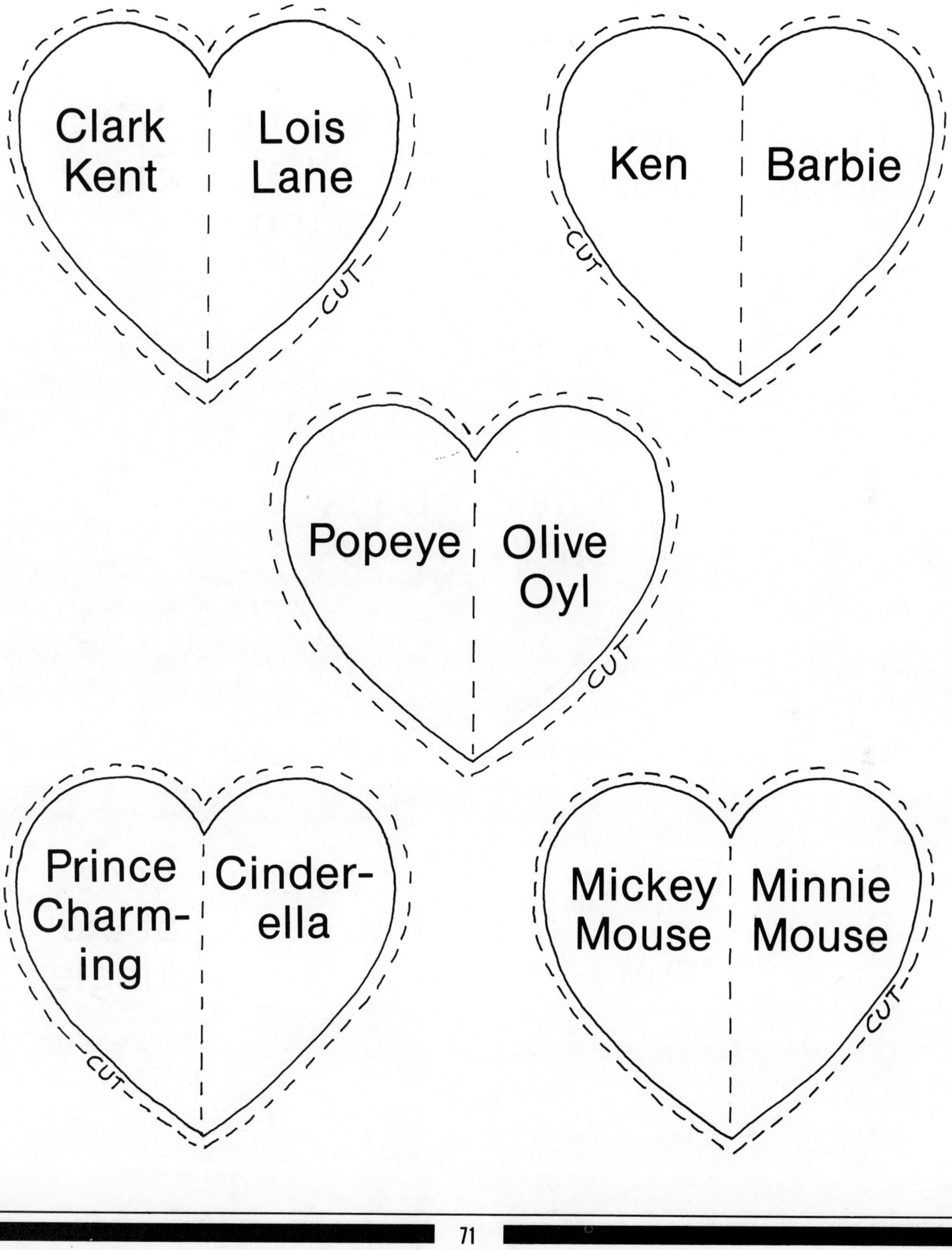

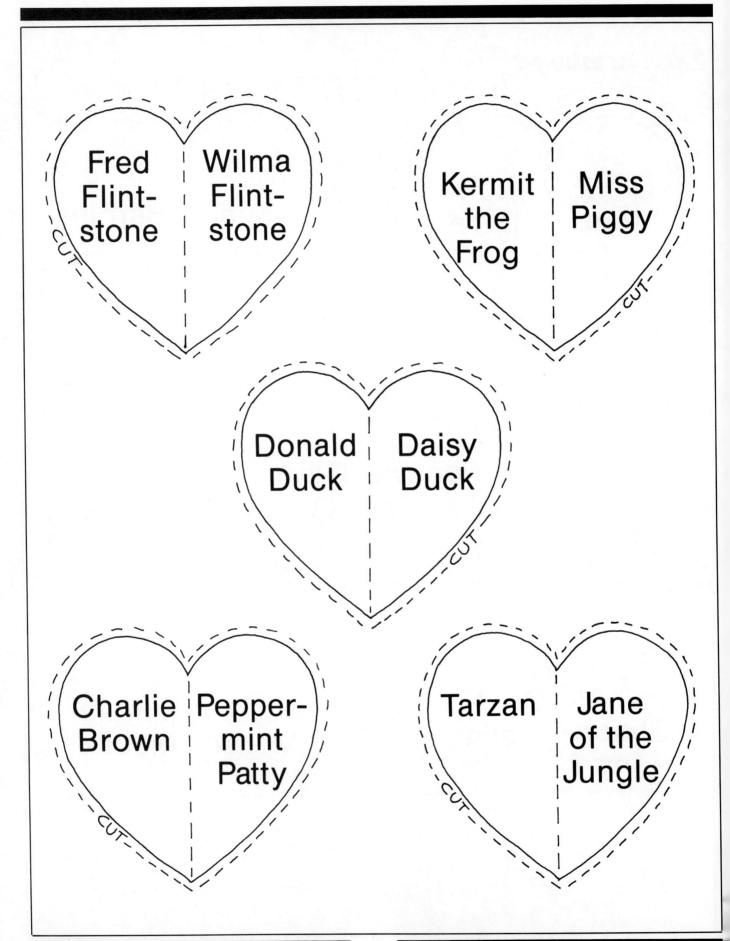

FAMOUS SAYINGS

PURPOSE: Students will practice using a thesaurus and a dictionary.

MATERIALS: Copy of the list of famous sayings
Small box or basket
Dictionaries
Thesauruses
Chalkboard and chalk

TEACHER PREPARATION:
1. Cut each famous saying from the list.
2. Fold each saying and put it in the box or basket.
3. Divide the class into small teams.
4. Give each team at least one dictionary and one thesaurus.
5. Provide the chalkboard and chalk.

STUDENT DIRECTIONS:
1. Each team draws two sayings from the box or basket.
2. Use the dictionary and thesaurus to look up each word in the sayings. Rewrite the sayings by changing each word to a different word. For example: "Flash, flash, petite asteroid" is another way to say, "Twinkle, twinkle, little star."
3. After the sayings have been rewritten, each team will try to stump the others. A member from one team writes a rewritten saying on the chalkboard.
4. Members of the other teams must guess the correct famous saying within two minutes.
5. If the other teams do not guess correctly within the time limit, the team tells the answer. The same team then challenges the others with its other rewritten saying.
6. If another team guesses the answer correctly, that team challenges the others with one of its rewritten sayings.

VARIATIONS:
*Have students work individually to rewrite the famous sayings. Then compare the various ways each saying was rewritten.
*Have teams rewrite each saying several ways.

LIST OF FAMOUS SAYINGS

A penny saved is a penny earned.

Every cloud has a silver lining.

He who hesitates is lost.

I may disagree with what you say,
but I will defend to the death your right to say it.

Life is just a bowl of cherries.

The best things in life are free.

A horse, a horse! My kingdom for a horse.

He who laughs last, laughs best.

I'm strong to the finish 'cause I eats me spinach.
I'm Popeye, the sailor man.

It's a bird; it's a plane; it's Superman!

A rolling stone gathers no moss.

What's up, Doc?

A bird in the hand is worth two in the bush.

Be my valentine.

An apple a day keeps the doctor away.

Jack Sprat could eat no fat; his wife could eat no lean.

'Tis better to have loved and lost than never to have loved at all.

Take me out to the ball game.

May the force be with you.

Make my day.

ST. PATRICK'S MEMORY GAME

PURPOSE: Students will use their visual memory skills.

MATERIALS:
2 copies of the memory cards
Markers
32, 3" x 5" cards
Scissors
Glue
1 copy of the student directions
Envelope

TEACHER PREPARATION:
1. Color the memory cards with markers, making two identical copies of each.
2. Cut out the memory cards and glue them to the 3" x 5" cards. Laminate them if possible.
3. Glue the copy of the student directions on the envelope.
4. Store the memory cards in the envelope.

STUDENT DIRECTIONS:
1. Three or four players may play.
2. Take all of the memory cards from the envelope and spread them out, facedown on the floor or a table.
3. The first player turns over two cards, one at a time.
4. If the cards match, the player keeps the pair and takes another turn by turning over two more cards.
5. If the cards do not match, the player must replace them facedown exactly where they were. All players try to remember what pictures were on the cards.
6. Players take turns until all of the pairs have been found and claimed.
7. The player with the most pairs wins the game.

VARIATIONS:
*Make four copies of the memory cards and have the students play a rummy game.
*Have the students prepare the memory cards.

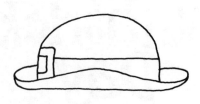

Erin-Go-Bragh

Happy St. Pat's Day

CATCH THE LIE

PURPOSE: Students will tell stories and demonstrate their acting skills.

MATERIALS:
Drawing paper
Markers
Scissors

TEACHER PREPARATION:
1. Have each student use the materials to draw and cut out a pot of gold.
2. Explain to the students that, according to legend, if you capture a leprechaun and keep your eye on him, he can't vanish. He might even tell you where his pot of gold is buried because this is how he tries to buy his freedom. But a leprechaun can never be trusted. He may tell you lies. Somehow leprechauns always manage to get away without paying.
3. Have the class choose a topic for discussion. For example, students might talk about "what I did last weekend."
4. Have each student find a partner.

STUDENT DIRECTIONS:
1. You and your partner will try to catch each other telling a lie like the legendary leprechauns.
2. You will take turns telling each other some facts about your topic. Each partner will talk for two minutes.
3. Watch carefully as your partner speaks because each person must include in this discussion a blatant lie. It is up to the other partner to catch the lie.
4. When you think your partner has told a lie, remember it. If you are correct, you may claim your partner's pot of gold.
5. If you are caught telling the lie, you must give up your gold to your partner.

VARIATIONS:
*Have each student write about the topic, trade papers with a partner, and underline the lie.

*Have some willing students try to fool the class.

MARCH MATH PROBLEMS

PURPOSE: Students will use reasoning skills to solve math problems.

MATERIALS: Copies of the March math problems
Pencils

TEACHER PREPARATION: 1. Divide the class into teams of four students each.
2. Give each team one problem.

STUDENT DIRECTIONS: 1. Your team will work together to solve the problem.
2. You may use any reasonable means to find the solution. It may be helpful to estimate an answer, work backwards, draw a picture or diagram, or look for a pattern. Like problems in real life, yours may include information that is not needed to solve the problem.
3. When all of the groups have finished, each group will share its problems with the class and show how the solution was found.
4. If two or more groups solved the same problem, compare the answers.

RALPH'S DAY OUT

Ralph was away from home on St. Patrick's Day for 8 hours. He had planned his day carefully. He got up early, put on his green jeans, his lucky shamrock, and the rest of his Irish-green clothes, and left home. He went to the museum for 1½ hours. From there Ralph went to the big parade downtown, and then he went shopping for 3 hours at the mall. If it takes Ralph 15 minutes to travel from each place to the next, how long did Ralph stay at the parade?

SPRING STRAWBERRY PIE

Lucy's Girl Scout troop has earned a lot of money selling strawberry pies each spring for four years. It is a perfect fund-raising project for the girls because they enjoy making the pies, and they have always sold every pie they made. This year they hope to make even more money than in past years. They have been collecting empty pie plates, so they won't have to spend any money on plates. The ingredients for the pies will cost about 55 cents each minus the strawberries. If they get a special deal on strawberries by picking their own, they figure that each pie will have 65 cents worth of strawberries in it. If they want to clear $150 this year, how many pies will they have to sell at $5.00 per pie?

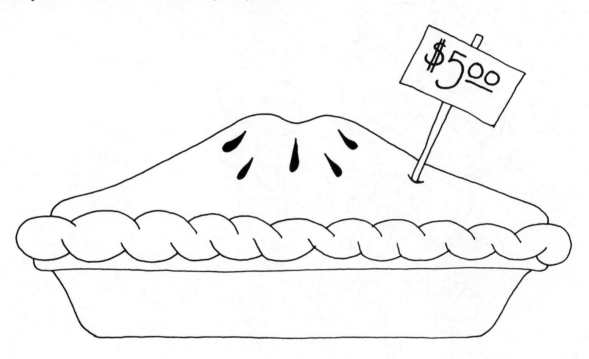

ST. PATRICK'S DAY PARTY

Four children were planning a St. Patrick's Day party. They planned all of the details and decided to share the expenses equally. Joe bought a cake with green frosting for $6.00 at the local bakery. Peggy bought $2.00 worth of green punch. Fred bought napkins with shamrocks on them for $2.00 and cups that matched the napkins for $1.00. Mary bought the mint ice cream for $5.00. How much did each child pay the others so that they each spent the same amount?

ST. PATRICK'S DICTIONARY HUNT

Name _____

Find the answers to these questions in your dictionary. Good luck!

1. St. Patrick is the patron saint of Ireland. On what page would you find *Ireland*? _____

2. According to Irish folklore, a leprechaun is a fairy in the form of a little old man who can reveal a buried crock of gold to anyone who catches him. What are the guide words on the page where the word *leprechaun* appears? _____

3. St. Patrick's Day is celebrated on March 17. What word comes before the word *March*? _____

4. *Shillelagh* is the old Irish word for a short oak club or cudgel. What is another way to spell *shillelagh*? _____

5. If a harp is colored green or has a sprig of shamrock, it is a symbol of Ireland. The harp played a part in Irish myths and legends. Is there a picture of a harp in your dictionary? _____

6. The green color of the grass, shamrocks, and all growing things had special meaning to the Irish long before St. Patrick. How many meanings can you find for the word *green*? _____

7. The shamrock, a clover with leaves in groups of three, is the emblem of Ireland. What are the guide words on the page where the word *shamrock* appears? _____

8. St. Patrick's Day is often celebrated with a parade. What is the foreign origin of the word *parade*? _____

9. St. is an abbreviation for the word *saint*. On what page will you find *St. Patrick*? _____

MAMA'S BABY

PURPOSE: Students will match descriptions of baby animals with their species.

MATERIALS:
1 pocket folder
Copy of the folder cover
Markers
Glue
Scissors
Copy of animal cards
16, 3" x 5" cards
Copy of the student directions

TEACHER PREPARATION:
1. Color the folder cover copy with markers. Glue it to the front of the pocket folder.
2. Cut out the animal cards and glue each to a 3" x 5" card. Mark matching colored dots on the backs of the cards to make them self-checking. Laminate the cards, if possible, and store them inside the pockets.
3. Glue the student directions inside the folder.

STUDENT DIRECTIONS:
1. Take out all of the animal cards.
2. Read the descriptions of baby animals on the cards. Match each description to the correct animal species.
3. When you have finished, look at the backs of the cards to make sure the colored dots match.

VARIATION:
*Have students research other animal babies and write additional sets of cards.

MAMA'S BABY

MAMA'S BABY ANIMAL CARDS

I'm a _____.	Description
I'm an elephant.	My pink baby is three feet tall at birth. In a few hours this 200-pound baby can stand, and in a few days it can walk with some help from me.
I'm a bear.	My newborn is about the size of a small rabbit. After three or four months it takes its first steps. I care for my baby for about a year, teaching it how to survive in the wild.
I'm a kangaroo.	My tiny baby is smaller than your thumb. It lives in my pouch for the first few months and hops in and out until it is ten months old.
I'm an alligator.	I build a nest in the mud and lay about fifty eggs. Then I seal the nest with mud and watch over it for about two months. After the eggs hatch, I tear open the nest with my teeth. Soon the babies are on their own.

I'm a frog.	Although I live in and out of water, my babies hatch from eggs under the water in the spring. They swim like fish until they are about two months old, when they get little legs. They are fully grown by summertime.
I'm a blue whale.	After about a year, my 25-foot-long infant is born. Unlike other mammals, my baby does not suck. I shoot a stream of milk into my baby's mouth when it's ready to eat.
I'm a trout.	I lay my eggs in a hole that I have carefully prepared at the bottom of a stream. After I cover up the hole with sand, I leave the eggs to develop on their own.
I'm an eagle.	I usually lay two eggs in my nest of sticks. When the babies are born, they are covered with dark feathers. Both parents help to feed them and later teach them to fly.

RABBIT ROBOT ROAD RALLY

PURPOSE: Students will work in teams and give directions.

MATERIALS: Copies of the Rabbit Robot Road Rally Instructions (one per student)

TEACHER PREPARATION:
1. On a playground or in the classroom, mark a starting point and a finishing point. Place a few obstacles, such as chairs or tables, between the points.
2. Divide the class into four teams—#1, #2, #3, #4.
3. Read the student directions to the class.
4. Give each student a copy of the Rabbit Robot Road Rally Instructions.
5. Act as referee for the activity.

STUDENT DIRECTIONS:
1. Each team must choose one member to be its robot. The robots cannot talk, and they can only move exactly as commanded by their team members.
2. Each team's goal is to direct its robot to move from the starting point to the finishing point in the least number of turns.
3. Team #1 begins by reading to the class the list of things its robot can and cannot do.
4. Keeping in mind those capabilities, team #1 then gives its robot a command to move from the starting point.
5. The race continues as each team takes its turn.
6. Robots along the course become obstacles for the other robots. In one command, a team may direct its robot to move forward or to turn but not both. (Example: "Take ten baby steps forward" or "Turn right three times.")
7. If a team gives a command that its robot cannot follow, the referee gives that team one more chance. If the command is still incorrect, the team loses its turn.
8. When one of the robots reaches the finishing point, its team wins.

RABBIT ROBOT ROAD
RALLY INSTRUCTIONS

ROBOT FOR TEAM #1:
Can hear only one command during the team's turn.
Moves forward in a straight line.
Can hop on only one foot.
Cannot turn left.
Stops when it touches anything.

ROBOT FOR TEAM #2:
Can hear only one command during the team's turn.
Moves forward in a straight line.
Takes only tiny baby steps.
Turns left when it touches anything and continues.

ROBOT FOR TEAM #3:
Can hear only one command during the team's turn.
Moves forward in a straight line.
Can take no more than three giant steps in one command.
Turns right after completing each command.
Stops when it touches anything.

ROBOT FOR TEAM #4:
Can hear only one command during the team's turn.
Moves forward in a straight line.
Can jump only with both feet.
Turns right when it touches anything and continues.
Cannot turn left.

EGGS IN A BAG

PURPOSE: Students will predict outcomes using probability and statistics.

MATERIALS: Copies of the two-page work sheet
For each pair of students:
4 plastic eggs, 2 each of two different colors
2 markers or crayons, the same colors as the eggs
2 pencils

TEACHER PREPARATION:
1. Have the students work in groups of four.
2. Provide the materials and verbally give the students their directions.
3. Give each student one copy of the work sheet.

STUDENT DIRECTIONS:
1. From your group of four, choose a partner to work with in the beginning.
2. Read the directions, follow them, and write your answers on the work sheet.

VARIATIONS:
*Substitute colored cubes, tiles, blocks, or squares of colored paper for colored plastic eggs.

*Extend the activity by:
● putting six eggs in the bag, three of one color and three of another color
● putting six eggs in the bag, two eggs each of three different colors

EGGS IN A BAG

Name _____

THE QUESTION:
You have four plastic eggs in a bag, two of one color and two of another color. If, without looking, you draw out two of the eggs, what is the probability that the two eggs will be the same color?

THE PREDICTION:
I think the probability is _____

_____

_____

_____

_____

THE POSSIBILITIES:
Color the eggs to show the possible combinations.

Tally:

1. _____

2. _____

3. _____

THE TEST:

Without looking in the bag, draw out two plastic eggs. Look at them. Have your partner tally the results next to the possibilities. Try this twenty-five times.

Next, you tally the results while your partner draws the eggs out of the bag twenty-five times.

THE GROUP STATISTICS:

After each member of your group of four has drawn out two eggs twenty-five times, compare the results.

Out of one hundred draws, _____

_____

_____

THE GROUP PREDICTION:

According to our group statistics, the probability of drawing two plastic eggs of the same color is _____

_____

_____

THE CLASS STATISTICS:

Compare results with the other groups. Out of all the draws in our class,

_____

_____

_____

THE QUESTION AGAIN:

You have four plastic eggs in a bag, two of one color and two of another color. If, without looking, you draw out two of the eggs, what is the probability that the two eggs will be the same color?

THE ANSWER:

Based on the results of the class, the probability is _____

_____

_____

SPRING SUNSHINE

MOTHER NATURE'S GAMEBOARD

PURPOSE: Students will gather natural materials and categorize them.

MATERIALS: 1 small bag for each student
Markers
Copy of the gameboard for each student
Heavy paper or poster board
Glue

TEACHER PREPARATION: 1. Glue each gameboard copy onto heavy paper or poster board.
2. Distribute the materials to the students.

STUDENT DIRECTIONS: 1. Using markers, decorate the bag with an outdoor scene.
2. Go outdoors and gather a variety of small natural items, putting them in your bag. (Examples: seeds, pebbles, feathers, twigs)
3. Back inside, take out each item. Find a word on the gameboard that describes it. Place the item in the space.
4. See how many spaces you can fill on the gameboard.
5. Glue the items into place.

VARIATIONS: *Students could pool the remaining collections and try to fill more boxes on their gameboards.
*Students could see how many words on the board fit each item in the collection.

MOTHER NATURE'S GAMEBOARD

shiny	white	hollow	brown
fuzzy	flat	prickly	hard
sticky	yellow	sharp	curved
light	moist	blue	round
red	soft	fluffy	dry
crumbly	long	pointed	smooth

CRAZY PHRASES

PURPOSE: Students will use clues to recognize phrases.

MATERIALS: 1 large envelope
Marker
Scissors
Copy of the phrase cards
Glue
10, 3" x 5" cards
Copy of the answer key
Copy of the student directions

TEACHER PREPARATION:
1. Use the marker to write "Crazy Phrases" on the front of the large envelope.
2. Cut out each phrase card and glue it to a 3" x 5" card. Laminate the cards, if possible.
3. Cut out the answer key and glue it to the back of the envelope.
4. Cut out the student directions and glue them to the front of the envelope.
5. Store the cards inside the envelope.

STUDENT DIRECTIONS:
1. Take out all of the cards.
2. Try to figure out what common phrase each card represents.
3. When you have done as many as you can, look at the answer key on the back of the envelope. Check your answers by matching the numbers on the cards to the numbered answers.

VARIATIONS:
*Have the students make up their own phrase cards.

*Have the students work in pairs, small groups, or teams to figure out the phrases.

*Make this a class activity by using an overhead projector and transparencies of the phrase cards.

1.

FAIRY

2.

take me

THE BALL GAME
THE BALL GAME

3.

horsing horsing horsing horsing horsing horsing horsing

4.

DU ⬇ MPS

5.

MARES

6.

T 👁 👁 L
T 👁 👁 L
★

7.

SISTER

8.

THE all FAMILY

9.

ANSWER KEY

1. Fairy tales
2. Take me out to the ball game
3. Horsing around
4. Down in the dumps
5. Nightmares
6. Twinkle, twinkle, little star
7. Stepsister
8. All in the family
9. Money doesn't grow on trees
10. Growing boy

10.

BOY

FUNTOONS

PURPOSE:	Students will write captions for pictures.
MATERIALS:	Pictures or cartoons Scissors Bulletin board Small cards Markers
TEACHER PREPARATION:	1. Collect pictures of animals and people, editorial cartoons, or newspaper comics. 2. Cut off and discard any captions or blurbs from the pictures. 3. Put one or more of the pictures on the bulletin board.
STUDENT DIRECTIONS:	1. Think of captions for the pictures on the bulletin board. 2. Use your imagination to make your captions clever. 3. Using markers, write your captions on the cards. Post the cards on the bulletin board.
VARIATIONS:	*Conduct a Funtoon Caption contest. Have the students vote on the best caption. *Hold a different Funtoon Caption contest each week. *Have the students bring pictures to class to use on the bulletin board.

SPRING A RIDDLE ON ME

PURPOSE: Students will match riddles with their answers.

MATERIALS:
1 large envelope
Copy of the envelope cover
Markers
Glue
Scissors
Copy of the student directions
Copy of the riddle cards
16, 3" x 5" cards

TEACHER PREPARATION:
1. Color the copy of the envelope cover with markers. Glue it to the front of the envelope.
2. Cut out the student directions and glue them to the back of the envelope.
3. Cut the riddle cards and glue each to a 3" x 5" card. Laminate the cards, if possible.
4. Store the cards inside the envelope.

STUDENT DIRECTIONS:
1. Take out all of the cards.
2. Read each riddle and match it to the answer that makes sense.
3. When you have finished, try out your favorite riddle on a friend.

VARIATIONS:
*Have the students make up riddle cards.
*Make a class booklet of riddles.

SPRING A RIDDLE ON ME

RIDDLE CARDS

Riddle	Answer
Why did the man plant bird seed?	He wanted to grow robins.
When is a horse like a bird?	When it's a horsefly.
What's the first thing you put in your garden in the spring?	Your foot.
What bug has a night-light?	A firefly.

What is in a lake but never gets wet?	Sunlight.
What has four legs and flies?	A cow in the summertime.
What animal splashes when it falls from the sky?	The rain, dear.
What do you call a family of eight baby cats?	Kitty litter.

Name _____

How many squares can you find? _____

How many triangles can you find? _____